Juv
932.021
BIA

$4

02 The unknown world at the bottom of the sea

04 Where the gods disappeared into the sea

06 Alexandria in 100 BC

08 A journey to Cleopatra's kingdom under the sea

22 Exploration on the seabed...

24 ... and what you will need

26 A diving adventure

30 Off to new horizons

33 The last voyage of the San Diego

36 Expedition to the San Diego

44 Who owns the treasure?

The unknown world at

- Seeing
- eye to eye
- with the
- Egyptian god Hapi

the bottom of the sea

At the bottom of the sea lie not only the hidden, mysterious worlds of plants and animals. Important relics from vanished civilizations – everyday items and objects of religious significance for those peoples; sailing ships; priceless treasure; temple complexes; and even entire cities have been lying for thousands of years at the bottom of the ocean.

And for thousands of years men have longed to explore the depths of the sea. Aristotle, the Greek philosopher and scientist, studied contraptions which would enable men to spend time underwater. It wasn't until 1538, however, that the first diving bell was actually introduced. For about 200 years now diving suits which completely cover the body have been available, enabling adventurers, bold explorers and scientists to study the seabed.

This book tells the story of Franck Goddio and his team. They have spent many years looking for, finding and raising treasures from the bottom of the sea all over the globe. Underwater archaeologists, who study ancient civilizations lost beneath the sea, examine and evaluate the finds. The information we already have from old documents and excavations is studied again and expanded in the light of new discoveries. New finds from the seabed are combined with familiar facts like the pieces of a jigsaw puzzle, in order to provide a complete picture of our history.

The two underwater projects described in this book tell of the treasures of Egypt which were lost at the bottom of the sea and of the wreck of the proud Spanish galleon, the *San Diego*. They, too, tell us about civilizations which have long since disappeared. Franck Goddio and his team invite us to accompany them in their exciting daily work, and to experience the difficulties and successes of a modern adventure, a mission full of surprises.

- An underwater rendezvous between the submarine and the archaeologists. Franck Goddio uses the submarine *Jules* during expeditions at great depths.

Where the gods disa

The Nile

is the longest river in Africa. It is made up of lots of little tributaries which rise deep in the heart of the scorching hot continent. After a journey of about 4,145 miles its lower reaches flow through the country of Egypt. And there, finally, it flows into the Mediterranean Sea in a massive, many-branched delta. On its long journey through the deserts of Egypt the fertile sediment he carries provide the Egyptians with a rich soil for their fields. It gives them the water they need to live, refreshing man and beast alike, and bears countless boats and ships to their destination. It is not surprising, therefore, that in addition to all the other gods in their temples and shrines, the ancient Egyptians should worship a deity dedicated to the River Nile's flooding. In the region around the Nile Delta this god was known as Hapi.

Alexander the Great – the founder of Alexandria

Over thousands of years the Old Kingdom of the Pharaohs, as the mighty kings of Egypt were called in those days, went into decline. Seafaring peoples from across the Mediterranean region began to take an interest in the wealthy country and its legends. They came across the seas in their ships on voyages of exploration and conquest. Many of them settled in the towns around the mouth of the Nile. In about 300 BC Alexander the Great, the Greek-Macedonian general, occupied the whole of Egypt. Having conquered the country he foundet a city and named it after himself: Alexandria. Unlike the other conquerors, however, Alexander did not destroy the ancient culture he found when he reached Egypt. He gained the support of many of the upper-class Egyptians and some of the ordinary people, but especially of the influential priests. He had himself crowned as Pharaoh. His successors, the Ptolemies, were to remain in power for about 300 years. Under their rule Alexandria

ppeared into the sea

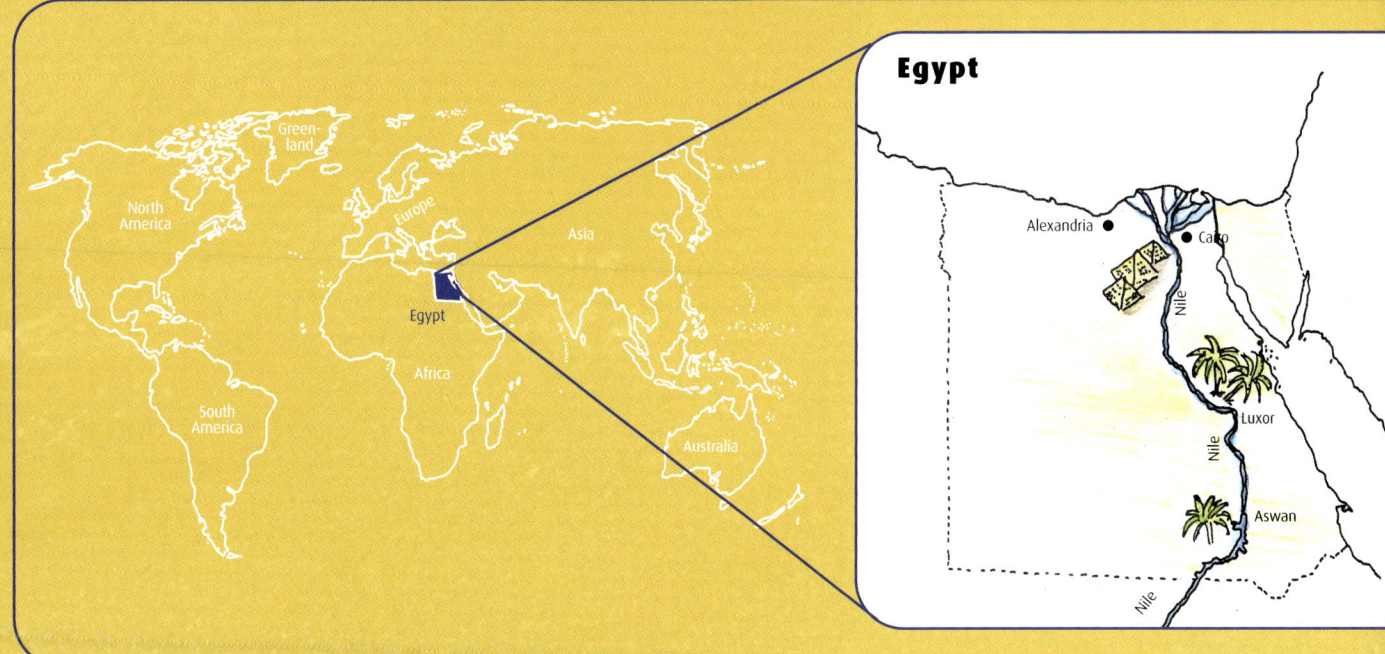

became the center of the Hellenistic – in other words the Greek – influenced world.

But the rapidly expanding Roman Empire had also set its sights on Egypt. It urgently needed the huge corn deliveries from the fertile Nile Valley for its vast armies, and the Romans also used the vast, fabulous deposits of gold from the kingdom of the Pharaohs to mint their new gold coins. And then there were the ports of the Nile delta, which were important not only as military bases for the navy. The magnificent royal capital of Alexandria was very important, especially as the trans-shipment point for goods and as a point of transition between the Mediterranean and the continent of Africa. Alexandria was a city worth gaining control of!

Cleopatra – the last great Pharaoh

Eventually the last great queen, Cleopatra, was unable to hold off the attacks from Rome any longer. Although she already had a son by the Roman consul Julius Caesar and even fell in love with the Roman general Mark Antony, in the year 30 BC, Cleopatra finally had to surrender her kingdom. From then on it was the Roman emperors who determined the fate of the land on the Nile.

Alexandria around

Government building

Royal port

Caesar's Temple

Royal port

Royal villa

Retirement villa of Mark Antony

Galley port

Herakleion approx. 19 miles

At second glance you will realize that the untidy heaps of stones lying in the shallow water are really sphinxes, columns and statues – and suddenly ancient Alexandria comes to life once more!

An enormous lighthouse called the Pharos indicated the safe route through the shallow water for ships entering the harbor. It was 394 – 459 feet high and was one of the Seven Wonders of the Ancient World. The ships sailed past it into a large basin consisting of several smaller ports, including the special royal harbor tucked away out of sight of curious onlookers. The rulers' warships could anchor there well out of sight. The main city port, by contrast, bustled with activity. Ships were loaded and unloaded, precious goods bartered, purchased and sold. From deepest Africa came valuable ivory, hardwoods, fragrant oils, exotic animals, animal skins, rare spices, gold and precious stones. Ships from Persia brought exquisite fabrics, pearls, silver, unknown plants and foodstuffs. Wine and oil arrived from Greece and metals from Spain. Sought-after marble from Italy was brought here to build new temples and magnificent buildings. There was an exotic mixture of fragrances of all kinds in the air. People called and shouted orders from ship to ship in strange tongues. Nowadays we would say that Alexandria was a modern, international city. There was a city wall to protect the city from intruders. The dead were buried outside the city walls. The district was called the necropolis, which means 'City of the Dead'.

And then there was the royal district with its magnificent palaces, temple complexes and shrines! It lay directly by the sea and had access to its own separate harbor. It was in this district that the most important library in those days was to be found. The entire knowledge of the world at that time was recorded in some 500,000 scrolls. Scholars and scientists came from far across the seas to exchange knowledge and experiences here.

From earliest times deities were worshiped in the temples and shrines. The people hoped that they would look on them favorably and grant them help and advice. The Ancient Egyptians, Greeks and Romans hoped to influence the gods in their favor with offerings, elab-

30 BC

Necropolis

Lighthouse

Pharos Island

orate processions and rituals, or they offered them thanks or requested help. They continued to worship the old Egyptian deities Isis, Osiris, Horus and Hapi, but also added Greek gods like Aphrodite, Zeus and Herakles to the list. As time passed, not only the people but also the cultures were blended with each other. Before long, in Alexandria there was a new common god for all religions: Serapis, the god of the underworld and of fertility.

Modern visitors to Alexandria will be astonished to discover that there is nothing left to see today of the relics of past times, of all the magnificent, elaborately decorated buildings! Gone, too, are the two legendary cities of Canopus and Herakleion, which ancient texts indicate must have been located to the east of Alexandria. We know that military campaigns and wars destroyed the region; that there were earthquakes; that the entire coastline collapsed; and that there were devastating floods. We know this because there have always been people who described the times in which they lived and wrote records of the important events of the time. Nowadays we would call them reporters or journalists. Some of

Serapis – Egypt's gods become Greek! Serapis not only united the different peoples who lived in Alexandria; he also united within himself the functions of god of the dead and the god of fertility. And he was also very popular as the god of healing.

their accounts have survived to the present day. Today, however, we also know a great deal thanks to computer investigations of the harbor and the immediate vicinity of the city of Alexandria. Enough unique discoveries await us here to fill an entire museum. What a challenge for scientists to study this mysterious world!

A journey to Cleopatra's

On that October day in 1997 the weather was bad. Dark clouds hung low in the sky, the wind was cold, and tall waves made the water choppy.

The divers in the harbor basin of Alexandria were waiting to start. Nowhere here is the water very deep – seldom deeper than 26 feet. That's just three times as deep as a swimming pool.
Sirens were hooting and there was bustling activity on all sides. Along the shore, vehicles of all kinds were zooming back and forth.
Below the surface of the water, the divers entered a world of total silence. Visibility was poor. Algae, mud washed up from the Nile, and industrial residues had polluted the water and made it cloudy. Suddenly the divers' lamps lit up a huge block of stone, and another one next to it. What looked at first like a rock was covered with slimy mud and sand. The movement of the waves and the divers' flippers swirled up even more sediment. The divers got out their scrapers and brushes, and suddenly there it was – the submerged

kingdom under the sea

statue of a sphinx made of gray granite. Here, at last, was a first mute witness of Egypt's past! And it would not be the last. Soon after that the divers found another sphinx. Once it had been cleaned it seemed to be thanking them for discovering it with an enigmatic smile.

Today we believe that one of four of the sphinxes that have been found to date bears the features of Ptolemy XII, Cleopatra's father. What a magnificent find! The divers were thrilled. The find was photographed underwater using a digital camera, and a waterproof label was attached describing exactly where it had been found. All the data were transmitted immediately to the base ship and fed into a database in the computer. The lengthy search which preceded this lucky find, the endless searching using sonar and other electronic equipment, suddenly seemed unimportant!

Gazing at a sphinx. Sphinxes are creatures from ancient times which are neither man nor beast: They have the body of a lion and a human head, usually male.

The statue of a lion was seen as the embodiment of power and strength. Pharaohs often had stone statues carved showing themselves wearing the royal head-dress, the nemes.

Like an avenue of trees these tranquil statues would flank the approach to the palaces and temples, for example the Temple of Karnak near Luxor shown here.

Cats were worshiped too. There was a cat goddess called Bastet. In the temples dedicated to her hundreds of little figures of cats were placed as offerings. They were supposed to make the goddess view the donor with favor. We learn from old texts that a Roman soldier was even beaten to death because he had killed a cat without reason!

A huge snake of granite coiled up and apparently sleeping peacefully on the seabed doesn't frighten anybody. We know its significance and even its name. It was called Agathodaimon and was worshiped as a benevolent spirit in houses and the city itself. In Alexandria the snake was thought to protect the inhabitants, bringing them good fortune and prosperity.

Animals as deities

In ancient Egypt many animals were regarded as sacred. Their nature was seen as divine.

The snake which coils itself around the Pharaoh's headdress – often represented in the form of a cobra – was a sacred creature.

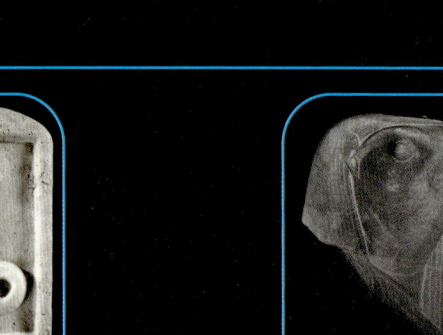

Head of a large flaconheaded sphinx, from of a particular god Hours

A bird frequently found in the Nile Delta, the ibis, was the god of knowledge and the art of writing.

A journey to Cleopatra's kingdom under the sea

The gods as rulers over the dead and protectors of the living

A few days later the divers came across a gray granite statue lying on the seabed. It looked as if it might depict a woman carrying a child. As always, at first it was impossible to see exactly because of the slime, mud and encrusted shells. Using brushes and scrapers the men carefully began to clean the layers away. Gradually a different picture emerged, and then they found themselves looking at something quite different: a man with a shaven head who was holding a vase with a head peering out of the opening. The man was wearing a tunica, the typical costume of Greco-Roman times. Fortunately the team consisted of experts from various different special fields! They had already set up a digital camera linked to the base ship via a cable. It quickly transferred the pictures to the experts waiting on board. Sitting in front of his computer screen, the archaeologist was soon able to solve the riddle: The bald-headed man was a priest from the temple of the goddess Isis. He was carrying a sacred object, a vessel known as a canopic jar containing the humours emanating from the body of Osiris. Only the god's head could be seen sticking out of the top.

Osiris and Isis, originally two Egyptian deities, were worshiped by both Greeks and Romans. There was a so-called Isis cult. In temples dedicated to the goddess Isis, priests with shaven heads performed rituals. Nowadays, in most religions, priests tend to wear a particular type of dress. In those days their distinguishing feature was their shaven head. Isis was worshiped as the mother goddess, the goddess of the dead and the protector of the living. She was said to have brought her brother Osiris, who was also her husband, back to life by putting his body back together again after he had been hacked into pieces. As a sign of her ability to overcome death the statue shows Osiris climbing out of the canopic jar and returning to life.

Continuing to search near where they had found the statue of the priest, the divers soon struck lucky again. Even on the seabed, objects which initially looked like nothing in particular emerged in the hands of the experts as relics of a glittering kingdom. A shipwreck, parts of the harbor installations, palaces, temples, tiled floors and tablets with Egyptian inscriptions, known as hieroglyphs, emerged. In Greek the word 'hieroglyphs' means 'sacred signs.' Nowadays they hold no secrets for us. Today we can read them and learn more about these times long past. It is as if we were looking at a newspaper made of stone. Might these discoveries possibly even belong to Cleopatra's royal villa? According to ancient reports it must have stood on a little offshore island near the harbor. However, the island, known as Antirhodos, has long since disappeared beneath the sea.

And then the divers found something very exciting indeed: A child's head made of stone with the features of Caesarion, the son of Caesar and Cleopatra!

Recovery and restoration

A royal prince emerges from the depths – the enormous head of Caesarion (= little Caesar), the son of Cleopatra and Caesar, has been secured and raised from the bottom of the sea.

Locating and finding the objects was just one part of the task in hand. Having fulfilled the first part of their mission, the restorers and conservators on board and later on land still had a great deal of work to do. The large items, such as statues and stone tablets, were carefully secured with ropes and slowly lifted to the surface using a crane. On the deck of the base ship chisels and small knives were waiting to be used. The experts removed the incrustations of shells and lime from the finds. Then they had to soak them to remove the salt – depending on the size of the objects, in small basins or a bath. Only then could the damage be seen properly. Whenever possible the broken sections were put back together again. If necessary they were replaced by other suitable materials. When necessary chemical substances were used to protect the works of art, or artifacts, in their new environment.

The objects were often too large and too heavy to be raised to the surface, or sometimes the experts wanted to decipher an inscription while they were still on the seabed. Modern technology makes such unusual requirements possible: an impression can even be made under water.

1 A large cloth is soaked in a special type of silicon.

2 Then it is laid over the surface of the inscriptions on the seabed, ...

3 ... weighted down with lead and firmly tied with ropes.

4 After an interval of up to 16 hours the plastic has hardened. The impression can be peeled off like a layer of skin.

A journey to Cleopatra's kingdom under the sea

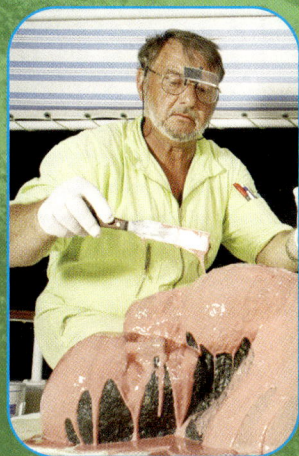 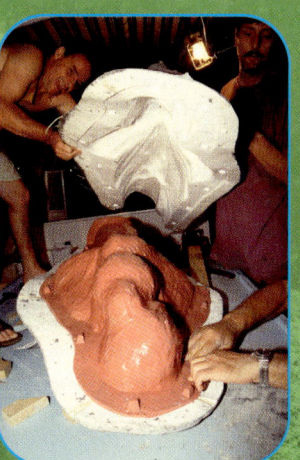 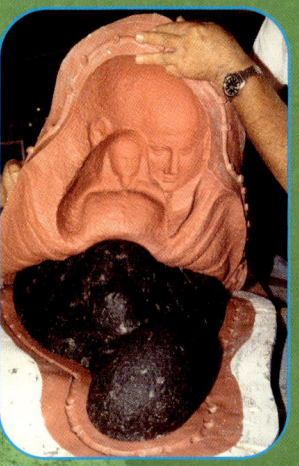 

1 The thick, elastic, rubber-like mass was brushed onto the front and back of the figure using a spatula.

2 After a certain amount of time the mass binds, in other words it becomes firm. You can make a negative impression in this way, like the impression of teeth a dentist makes for a brace.

3 The two halves of the form are put together. Then they are filled with synthetic resin or another suitable material.

4 In this way it is possible to produce an exact copy of a real statue, a so-called replica, which means approximately 'repetition'.

A museum under the sea?

The statue of the priest with the canopic jar was lifted back up into the daylight once more. Once it had been cleaned it was given a special treatment, because the experts wanted to make an impression of it. They had all the equipment they needed on board.

And then, something remarkable happened: After impressions had been made of all the big, heavy statues and all the data had been stored, they carefully slid the finds back down again into the gloomy depths of the harbor of Alexandria. The sphinxes and the priest of Isis were put back in a selected location in a quiet, safe place. There, on the seabed, they were to wait until further decisions had been made, because the researchers had some bold plans for the future. An underwater museum, maybe? By doing this they were leaving the options open for new, pioneering ideas. Who knows? Maybe one day they will even become reality.

Submerged priest – Until a decision has been made as to where he is to be preserved in future, the priest of Isis is waiting, 'watched over' by two sphinxes, in a safe place at the bottom of the sea.

Aboukir

Some time was to pass before Franck Goddio could report further finds. He had been studying another area described in old texts, the region known today as the Bay of Aboukir. It lies about 22 miles away to the northeast of Alexandria. Today Aboukir is a military and fishing port. In ancient times, however, the Nile must have split into arms. The towns of Herakleion and Canopus are thought to have been situated where an arm of the river flowed into the Mediterranean. Herakleion was a large, important customs and trading port. That was only the case, however, until Alexander the Great founded Alexandria in 331 BC. After that Herakleion rapidly declined in importance, and Alexandria became the new gateway to Egypt for seafaring nations and traders alike. Canopus is described as the town of temples. Egyptians, Greeks and Romans went on pilgrimages to the shrines of Isis and Serapis there. They hoped that a miracle would cure them of disease or pain – like present-day pilgrims traveling to a shrine. The region to be explored was very large. The search there would prove to be time-consuming and difficult. Electronic surveys had already been undertaken and numerous underground maps drawn up.

All new discoveries, their location and dimensions were marked on the maps. Gradually it is possible to reconstruct a plan of the submerged cities with their harbour, temples and imagine them.

Canopus

Herakleion

Reconstruction of the former coastline between Alexandria and Herakleion. Herakleion and Canopus lie up to 4 miles from the present coastline, sunken beneath the sea.

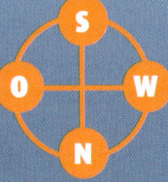

A journey to Cleopatra's kingdom under the sea

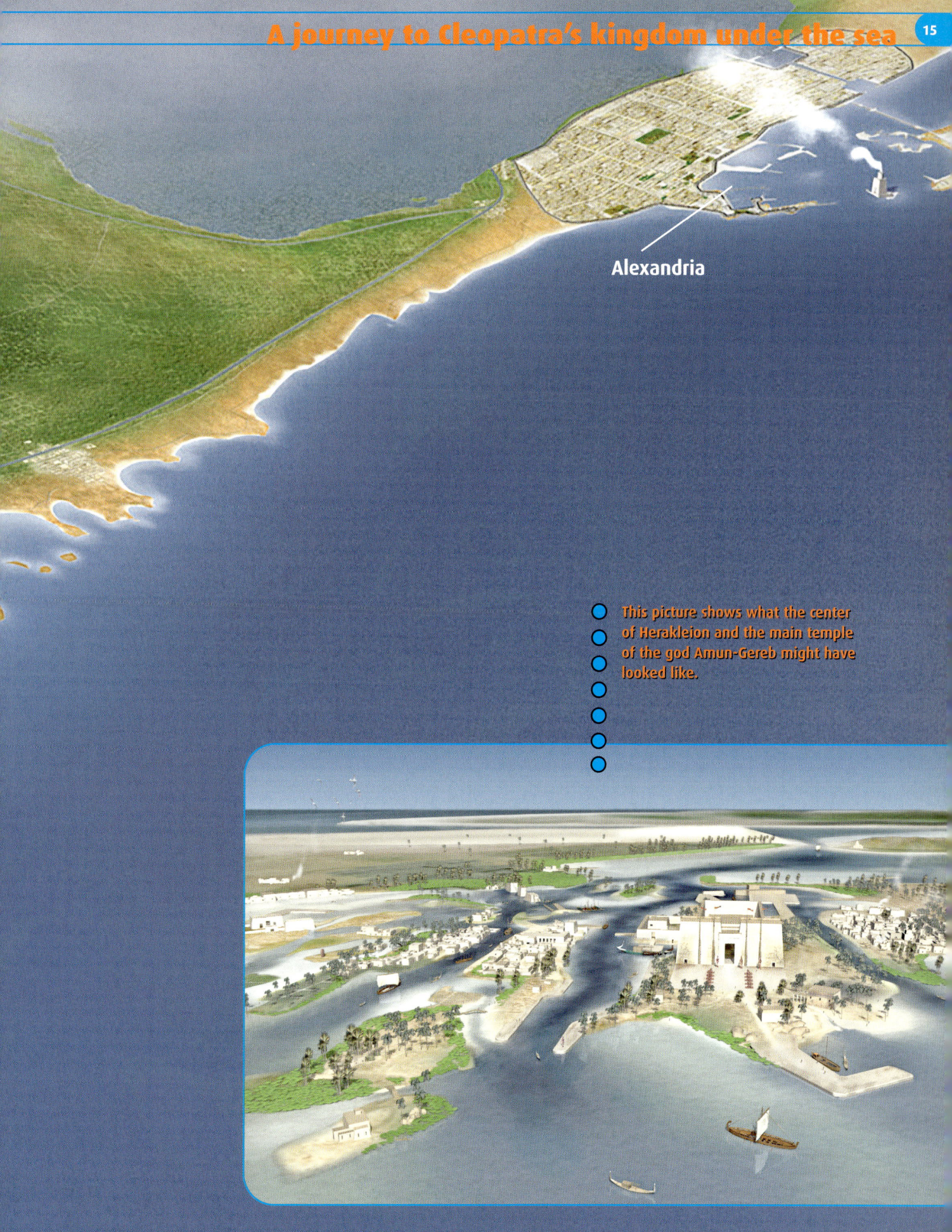

Alexandria

This picture shows what the center of Herakleion and the main temple of the god Amun-Gereb might have looked like.

The treasure of Aboukir

Finally Franck Goddio's team succeeded in finding a field of ruins beneath the sea. The first diving expeditions brought new finds to the surface. The remains of an old port and ten submerged shipwrecks lay at the bottom of the sea! It might indeed be the ancient port of Herakleion.

It was a tremendous challenge for the divers, because once again visibility was very poor in the milky-green water. Floating particles of algae and sediment swirled around in front of the divers' masks. And then there were the ruins of what was left of the walls, which confused them as well and kept leading them the wrong way. It is all too easy to lose your sense of direction under water! Fortunately they could use their compasses to help them sort out where they were. And then suddenly: Behind a fallen column they found coins, vases and jewelry, all buried beneath the sand.

Only when all the locations where objects were found had been recorded could the divers pack the treasures into the nets and nylon bags they had brought down with them and bring them back to the surface. There the archaeologists, restorers and conservators were waiting for fresh tasks.

In the cloudy water the divers suddenly found themselves in front of a wall consisting of huge limestone blocks. It was the wall surrounding a huge temple which was over 330 feet long.

The emperors' gold. Objects found on the seabed are usually covered in a thick layer of concretions – except for those made of gold. Gold coins gleam even after centuries under water almost as brightly as on the day they were minted.

A journey to Cleopatra's kingdom under the sea

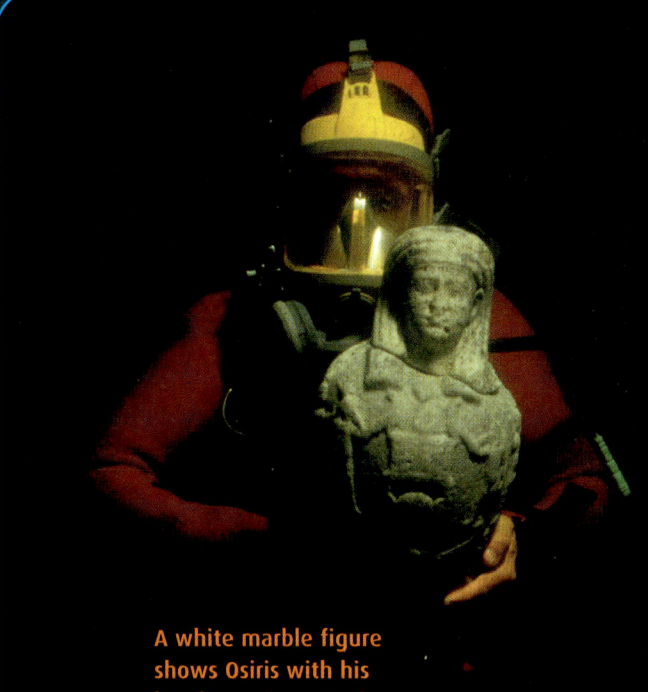

A white marble figure shows Osiris with his head peeping out of a canopic jar.

A diver checks over a small figure. It is a bronze statue of the goddess Bastet in the form of a cat.

Once again they carefully use a soft paintbrush to reveal the surface details.

Then more digital photos are made and sent back to the base ship along with all the important data.

•••••• Cleaned of algae and dead shellfish, Serapis gazes confidently into the future. Will Franck Goddio and his team find the rest of the statue, which might have been 13 – 15 feet high?

A journey to Cleopatra's kingdom under the sea

Piece by piece the huge statue emerges from the water. First to appear are the hands with the sacrificial table.

Hapi, the god of the Nile flooding and fertility, has been resting at the bottom of the sea for two thousand years. As he emerges from the greenish water into the broad daylight he seems to smile with pleasure.

Near the god of the Nile's flooding, Hapi, Franck Goddio's team has also found a statue of Isis. With their height of 16 feet and weight of about 5 tonnes they really are colossal statues.

The twilight of the gods

For weeks the scientists continued to dive in the Bay of Aboukir, and time and again they came across surprising finds. In the middle of the jumble of massive stone blocks a white marble head with a beard and curly hair suddenly rose to meet them. On closer examination it turned out to be the remains of a big statue of the god Serapis. Once upon a time it was worshiped in its temple in Canopus, before being destroyed at some point and then forgotten for a very, very long time. The team continued to work feverishly. Every day they discovered more treasures. They discovered a *naos* made of pink granite. They were able to rescue an enormous statue, also of pink granite – a very popular stone for buildings and artifacts. The statue represented Hapi, the god of the Nile's flooding.

A *naos* is the shrine housing the holy of holies in an antique temple. It was here that the cult statue of the principal god to whom the temple was dedicated was kept.

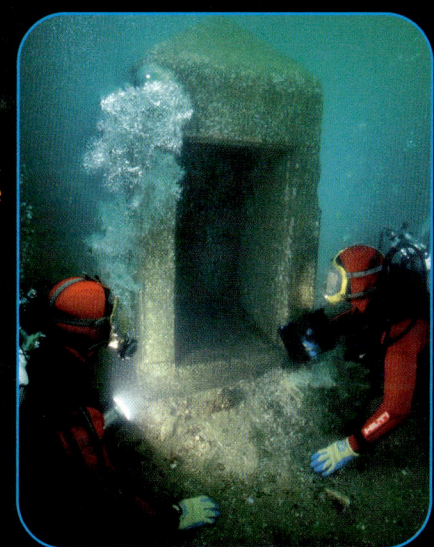

Stones can speak

The find of a stele of dark gray granite must have been a real bombshell!
We know that in Egyptian times important laws and decrees were engraved in stone. Reports of the Pharaoh's successful military campaigns and other important events were also recorded on steles. These huge stone blocks were erected in important locations such as city gates, port entrances or in front of temples. That meant that everyone could see them.
It seems incredible, but the stele which Franck Goddio's team found was completely undamaged and in excellent condition. The Egyptologists could decipher without difficulty the news of 380 BC – at least those items of news which were important enough to be engraved in stone:

Amongst other things they read that Greek merchants and craftsmen were permitted to settle here in Thonis! And Thonis was the old Egyptian name for Herakleion! Like a piece of a jigsaw puzzle this find finally seemed to fit in with the old reports. It forms part of the picture of the important ancient port and trading city which bore the double name Herakleion – Thonis, and which once flourished at the mouth of a long-submerged arm of the Nile.

The research project in Alexandria and its surroundings was finished for the moment, but the mission as a whole was far from over: There are still plenty of new things waiting to be discovered in the former Nile delta!

A journey to Cleopatra's kingdom under the sea

Important news from times long past!

Almost 6 feet 7 inches high, the granite stele is carefully lifted by crane from the seabed onto the research ship *Princess Duda*.

After it has been carefully cleaned and placed in a huge bath to remove the salt, and other necessary work has been completed, the experts examine the elaborately carved stone.

Silicon impressions make the inscriptions legible. This technique is used not only under water but also once the object has been brought on board ship. Everyone was very excited to learn what the inscription said and no one was prepared to wait until all the important Egyptologists had had time to examine the stele in person. And so they quickly made an impression, transformed it into a digital picture and sent it to the experts to be deciphered.

Exploration

Even when the lighting conditions are optimal you can scarcely read the inscriptions at the bottom of the sea. Fortunately, however, it is also possible to make silicon impressions of the inscriptions under water, thus enabling the hieroglyphs to be deciphered quickly.

Diving into the secrets of our past. There is still plenty of work on the seabed for the underwater archaeologists.

Underwater archaeology is still a very young science: it has only existed since the mid-twentieth century. Rapidly advancing technology now makes it possible to locate objects under water with great precision. And excavation methods which are suitable for use on the seabed have been developed too. For example, there is waterproof paper and writing tools for quick sketches, silicon substances for precise impressions, and chemicals and precision tools for the careful removal of unwanted incrustations from delicate finds.

Among the everyday equipment used by underwater scientists are electronic maps of the seabed, computer technology, GPS positioning, and cameras which operate at a great depth. On the seabed you can scarcely read the inscriptions, even when the lighting conditions are optimal. Fortunately, however, it is even possible to make a silicon impression of inscriptions under water in order to allow for the hieroglyphs to be deciphered without delay. And there are remote controlled underwater vehicles. They take over difficult and dangerous tasks for the divers.

Nonetheless, the cooperation between Franck Goddio and his numerous assistants in the research team is far from routine. A large crew of experienced sailors is required to operate a research ship with all its technical apparatus. And then they need divers with special training, cameramen and scientists including archaeologists, conservators and restorers. Conservators are responsible for the preservation of old objects; they protect them from further decay. Restorers attempt to return damaged objects to their original condition. They can only hope to achieve their ambitious goals if they all work together: And that is to discover treasures from past civilizations in the sea, to bring them back into the light of day, and to make them available for the public to enjoy in their original splendor.

on the seabed...

Underwater photography is a particular challenge for photographers. For example, they must bear in mind that the water filters the light in a different way and that the pictures will tend to have a greenish or bluish tinge.

Here the measurements are being recorded on a plastic slate covered with a sheet of polyester.

The real treatment of the find starts on the surface. First of all the object is freed from sediments, for example using a paintbrush and a scraper.

The conservator's meticulous work continues in the workshop. For example, a metal object can be cleansed of salt by using an electrochemical process.

... And what you

Archaeologists at work – they are using a brush to clear away the marine incrustations on the face of a colossal statue.

Using an excavation grid made of steel cables and a measuring tape, an archaeologist records the exact position of a find on the seabed.

A sort of vacuum cleaner can be used to remove loose sand.

Under water

Once they have defined an area, archaeologists on land and in the water use the same system in order to examine a location precisely. They draw up what is known as an excavation grid. They divide an area into square fields using ropes, cables or wires which are anchored to the ground with pegs. The result is a sort of enormous chess board. Or you could also imagine it as a town plan which has been divided into squares. The areas, thus individually marked, can be studied in any order. At the end you will have a large complete picture again.

Powerfull water dredges to remove the sediment function rather like the vacuum cleaner we use at home. Particularly useful are picks, scrapers and steel brushes made of non-rusting material. They help to remove the concretion from the finds. Concretions are residues on objects or on the ground. Over the course of many years they can built up a kind of encrusted shells around the objects.

will need

Above water

If the depth of the water permits, the base ship can lie carefully anchored above the site of the excavation. As a research ship it is equipped with the latest technology. It has strong compressors so that the divers' air bottles can be filled, and there is even a crane to raise the objects to the surface. The data is regularly transmitted to the archaeologists on the boat and integrated in the computer database.

Sonar equipment is essential. Sonar picks up sound signals which are transmitted to the seabed and bounce back. It then displays on a screen the irregularities and high and low spots on the ground.

On board, apart from the captain, you will find the sailors, mechanics, electronics engineers and lots of helpers. They have come together from all the corners of the globe. They are the specialists who together form the crew of the research ship.

Life is comfortable on the ship – it is almost like being in a little self-contained town. There is a television to watch films. There is a cook to prepare the food. Every day he prepares delicious meals and bake fresh bread. Even a doctor can be on board to ensure the additional safety of the crew. Who knows? Maybe someone will suddenly develop toothache or an accident may occur and require rapid medical assistance. During the entire expedition the base ship becomes the home of the crew members, who may number as many as 30.

The research ship *Princess Duda* with a dinghy and a barge for large finds.
All the data from the underwater investigations are stored in the computer center on board.

A diving adventure

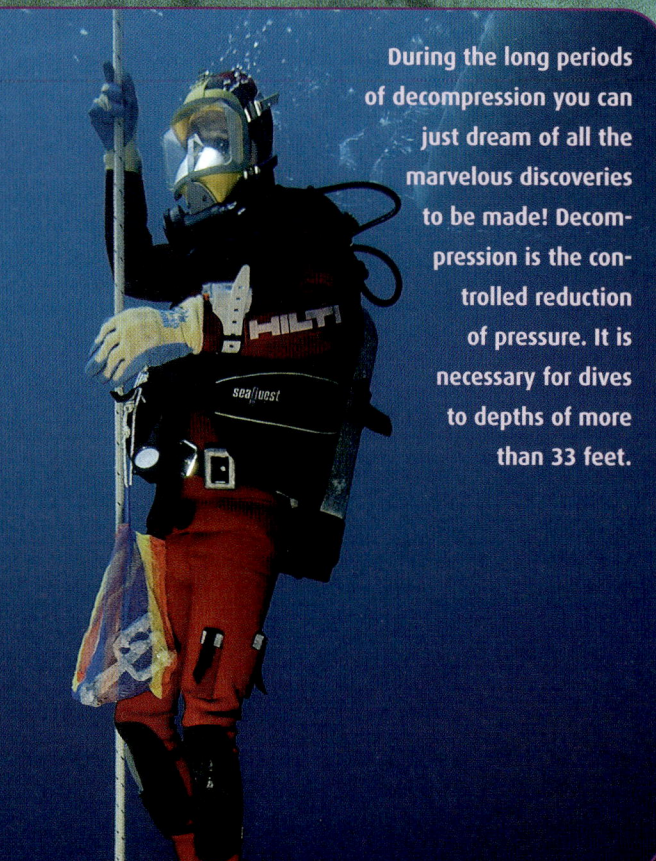

During the long periods of decompression you can just dream of all the marvelous discoveries to be made! Decompression is the controlled reduction of pressure. It is necessary for dives to depths of more than 33 feet.

If you want to take part in an expedition on the seabed you will have to overcome many obstacles, because you will be operating in an alien environment.

The first requirement for operating under water is that you know how to dive. Each dive is a time-consuming undertaking and the human body finds it hard to cope with the increasing pressure at depth. You must be an experienced diver and apart from being fit and agile you must have a good archaeological training. You must be used to working in a team and you must be able to make decisions quickly and reliably. Work under water is frequently made more difficult by poor visibility and strong currents. These dangerous currents constantly change the layout of the seabed. They carry away submerged objects and can heap up high mountains of sand in just a few years. Objects often do not remain in the same place unless they are very heavy. They are carried away – if you are lucky, onto the shore. Sometimes smaller objects get caught up in fishing nets and surface again in this manner.

Diving equipment – technology for surviving under water

In this world full of secrets and surprises we humans have to wear specially adapted clothing. The diver must be able to breathe, see and swim. A diving suit made of synthetic neoprene fabric protects him from the cold and minor injuries. You can move in it and yet it is very tough. In particular, it helps the diver to maintain his body temperature. Gloves, a helmet and boots are made of the same material. The face is protected by a mask. The masks are made and adjusted individually for each diver in the team. They are completely watertight, they keep warm and protect the skin during the long dive.

An electronic intercom system is built into the mask and connected to the base ship on the surface. Air for breathing is supplied through one or two cylinders of compressed air. As the name suggests, the air in the cylinders has been compressed. A full air cylinder contains about as much air as would fit into ten bathtubs. Big pumps called compressors have forced the air into the steel cylinders. The diver straps them onto his back on top of his jacket. Then, by using a diving regulator he can breathe in and out normally. During a dive the diver must keep a constant check on how much air he still has left. To do this he needs to keep an eye on his manometer. This is linked to the air cylinder by a tube and measures the pressure inside the cylinder. The lower the pressure, the less air is left in the cylinder. A medium-sized bottle is sufficient for a dive of about two to four hours. If you want to dive you will also have to weigh yourself down in order to be able to sink in the water. With stones? No, the diver wears a belt made of

lead weights. His diving jacket is very important when he returns to the surface. It is linked with the compressed air cylinder and has a valve by means of which it can be filled with air. Then the diver seems to get lighter so that he can return to the surface again. The jacket also supplies enough buoyancy to permit him to keep his balance when working in the water.

The divers shine lights into even the smallest crannies so that they can explore them. After all, they might contain untold treasures.

Franck Goddio's team consists of experienced divers. They have completed so many dives that they almost forget that they are moving around on the seabed and not on dry land.

The underwater archaeologists search for buried treasure with various types of detection equipment.

The diver must always know his exact diving depth at all times, because his air consumption rises with increasing depth. What is more, it can be fatal to dive to depths below 131 feet. Normal air can make the diver sleepy at depths below 131 feet. He will then behave as if he is drunk. This phenomenon is known as the "rapture of the deep" or nitrogen narcosis. If you need to dive to greater depths than this you will need a different mixture of gas and air in your compressed air cylinders. The depth gauge is fixed to the diver's arm where it can be clearly seen, like a watch.

The deeper the diver sinks, the greater the weight of water pressing on him, because water is heavy. If the human body were hollow he would soon be crushed. However, this is not the case, and so it is only the internal organs which are pressed together, especially the lungs and the air they contain. If you surface quickly the air, which has been compressed in your lungs, expands too rapidly. This can rip delicate organs apart, especially the lungs. And so the body has to adjust gradually to the reduced pressure. The diver must surface slowly, with prescribed pauses, as he gradually returns to the surface. This process is known as decompression. People move very slowly under water. A diver can only use his arms and legs to move. He has no fins like all the creatures which are able to swim fast under water. And so, for about 70 years now, divers have put rubber flippers on their feet or on top of their diving shoes. These help them to move about more easily in the water.

Other items of equipment include a knife, a compass and a lamp. You might need the knife to cut yourself free from floating fishing nets or to cut through wires which may be in the way. The compass is for orientation and shows the diver the direction in which he must swim. And then, finally, the lamp is used to light up things which cannot be seen clearly in the murky water. It is needed to enable the divers to recognize and read inscriptions and signs.

And last but not least, the divers have nylon nets and plastic bags of various sizes attached to their belt. These can be used to carry smaller finds to the surface. With all this equipment a diver can embark on the adventure of gliding down into the twilight world of the sea.

A diving adventure

Just one big leap and the diver is on his way into the exciting underwater world.

Checking your diving equipment is one of the most important tasks on board. The divers' lives depend on it being in good working order.

In the endless depths of the sea the link to the base ship provides an element of security.

Off to new horizons

Christopher Columbus's main achievement was discovering the New World – America – in 1492.

Manila, the hub of seaborne trade. The Spanish were successful sailors and merchants who soon aroused the envy of other seafaring nations.

The Philippines are not just a single land mass. They consist of thousands of tiny islands and archipelagoes. Manila has been the capital since 1571. The Philippines have a tropical climate. That means that the humidity is very high and the heat is almost unbearable. The seasons are governed by heavy rainfall: we talk of the rainy season or the monsoon season. Violent storms, dangerous typhoons and unpredictable hurricanes can also whip across the islands, leaving behind them a trail of destruction.

Since the 16th century the whole of Europe had been caught up in a spirit of optimism. Columbus had discovered America! The great seafaring nations such as Spain, Portugal, France, England and Holland set off to find new, better sea routes and to explore regions they had never sailed to before. On behalf of the crown, in other words in the name of the king of the country concerned, the sailors took possession of the countries they discovered. They declared them as colonies. Raw materials and mineral resources like gold, silver, gems and crops belonged immediately to the mother country. In time there was something resembling a competition between these bold seafaring countries. Each one wanted to own as many colonies as possible.

From the mid-16th century the Philippines were Spain's farthest colony. They enabled the mother country to control and profit from the trade between Asia, America and Europe. They charged customs duties and other fees for ships which wanted to unload their cargoes in Manila. The money went to the colonial overlords, which meant the King of Spain. The Philippines had no mineral resources of their own, but the country was ideally located to become a hub for valuable goods from faraway lands.

Off to new horizons

Heavy seas often gave the sailors a very rough time. A shipwreck was a catastrophe to be avoided at all costs.

Strategically speaking, a favorable location is when a large number of people have to make use of certain specific services at a particular place. For example, if after a long voyage you can moor your ship on an island where there are supplies of fresh water, fresh food and other provisions, you would be well advised to do so. That was the case with Manila. Situated not far from Japan and opposite China, Manila developed into a focal point for trade between Asia and the American continent. And from America to Spain via the Azores it was not very much further either. And so it is not at all surprising that the city of Manila, and thus the motherland Spain, gradually became richer and richer over the years.

Japanese and Chinese junks brought shimmering silks, rare spices, tea and household goods made of finest blue and white porcelain. They traded fabrics of delicate cotton for Asian foodstuffs, dyes and gloss paints. When they set sail again for their native land the junks were not empty, of course. In Manila the Chinese merchants took on board items such as pieces of silver, because strangely enough the Chinese valued that precious metal more highly than gold. The silver had been extracted in the silver mines of the American continent, in New Spain – the country we call Mexico today. The precious freight set sail across the vast ocean towards Manila in the holds of a Spanish galleon from the port city of Acapulco. That is why the galleons were also known as "silver ships."

The perils of a sea voyage

In those days a sea voyage was full of hardships and deprivation. You could never be sure whether the ship and its crew would arrive back safely. There were countless dangers along the way. Pirates frequently attacked and plundered the ships, because it was always worthwhile to capture a fully-laden ship with its valuable cargo. There were violent storms: in the tropics, typhoons often caused shipwrecks. Nobody had reliable maps of the sea. The captain and his sailors were utterly helpless in the face of treacherous currents and razor-sharp reefs below the water's surface. Such events could lead to an entire ship being lost with all hands. And then there were accidents at sea, epidemics and disease resulting from polluted drinking water, or the crew could even die of thirst. The drinking water supplies were always very meagerly calculated; in the tropical heat, the fresh water often went bad, or sometimes the supplies ran out. Scurvy was one of the many diseases the sailors dreaded. It develops because humans are not able to store sufficient vitamin C in the body. Vitamin C is found in fresh fruit and vegetables – but that is precisely what was no longer available after a few weeks at sea! In those days all sailing ships were made of wood. In warm waters there is a particular worm which bores into the planks and wooden parts of the ship under water and eventually makes a hole. Rather like the woodworm with which we are familiar, these worms can even consume an entire ship. The captain, not knowing what to do, found himself watching what was happening without being able to do anything about it!

The junk was a large sailing ship from Asia with a shallow draft designed for use on both rivers and the sea. Another typical characteristic of the junk was its sails of bamboo or rice matting which were subdivided into sections by wooden battens, rather like blinds.

Galleons were one of the most successful types of sailing ship; they had been built in Spain and Portugal since the mid-16th century. They were distinguished by the figurehead jutting out on the bow.

The last voyage of the San Diego

As the galleon sails out of the bay its sails are not yet fully set. But the crew have already climbed into the shrouds to set the mainsail as well.

For days now the huge sailing ship had been becalmed, bobbing up and down on the windless ocean. The wooden deck planks creaked; with every movement of the waves the sheets and sails, hanging loosely down, crashed alarmingly against the masts and the deck superstructures.

On deck it was unbearably hot. The entire crew had already capitulated in the face of the stifling tropical heat. With sweat pouring over their bodies, the men struggled to complete their daily tasks. Every day the scorching hot planks had to be scrubbed down with sea water. That meant hours of exhausting work on hands and knees. Now the crew had time to attend to repairs: a damaged sail here, a worn rope there, and broken pieces of wood elsewhere. They were still faced with the prospect of a long, dangerous voyage – six to eight months at sea! Would they reach their destination, the port of Acapulco, safe and sound? Who would pay with his life for the voyage this time?

The holds

were full of goods of every description. The elegant Spanish citizens of New Spain demanded such luxuries and were prepared to pay high prices for them.

They still had enough food and drinking water on board. Before setting sail in Manila they had brought live animals on board: four pigs, four sheep, and a large number of hens. In this way fresh meat could be guaranteed, at least for the first part of the journey. Weather permitting, they could go fishing as well – what a feast! The basic foods on board included ship's biscuits and rice, served with cooked dried vegetables, or pulses such as lentils, peas and beans. Olives, garlic, onions and nuts were also stored in earthenware pots and pitchers. Perishable foods were air-dried on land in Manila, or they could be smoked, salted or pickled in vinegar. They still had enough fresh drinking water to cook the rice, and the ship's biscuits had not yet been infested by weevils. This luxurious state of affairs could change very quickly! Then the daily portions would start getting smaller, and not long after that the crew would start to show signs of malnutrition.

It was always dark. Only the entry hatches when they were open admitted a pale shimmer of light down below and allowed a little fresh air to enter.

The sailors' few possessions were quickly stowed away in chests. They might be souvenirs of home, perhaps a rosary or a lucky religious medallion.

The hammocks swung side by side under the low wooden ceiling. These were the sleeping quarters of the sailors. Before long, their bedding and clothes were full of vermin. They were easy prey for fleas and other parasites. It was not just that these unwelcome guests passed on various diseases. Together with worms and maggots, not to mention mice and rats, they also ruined the precious food supplies. They were a constant plague of life at sea. The captain was somewhat luckier. His living quarters were located in a superstructure mounted on the stern, the rear part of the ship. The captain's cabin was fitted out with proper furniture, glass windows and all the equipment and instruments needed for navigation at the time.

A fateful encounter

The *San Diego* had already crossed the Pacific Ocean twice without suffering any serious damage. Now the ship was waiting in Manila again before setting off on another crossing. But this time the outcome would be different! For a long time now the Dutch had been eyeing the wealthy Spanish colony of Manila greedily, and for weeks a Dutch ship, the *Mauritius*, had been

Life on board

was bearable in spite of the stifling heat – except below decks, where the air was stuffy and the smells of perspiration and the dung of the live animals almost took your breath away. There was no way of ventilating the area, because here, in the belly of the ship, there were no windows.

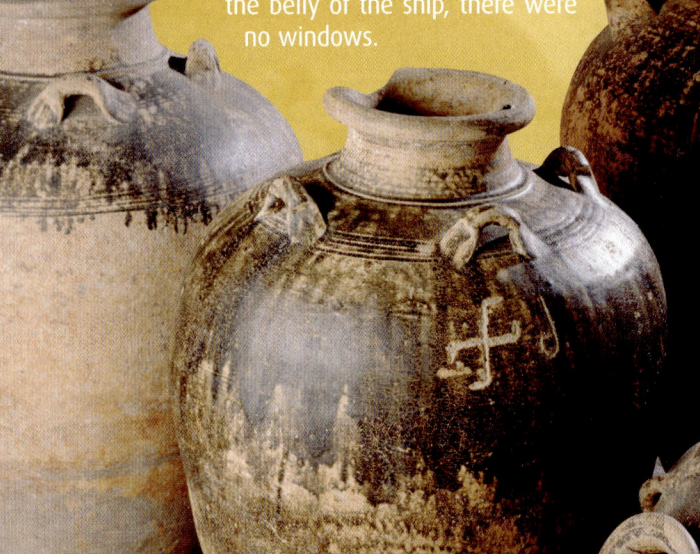

Pitchers were used to store foodstuffs as well as gunpowder, which was needed for the cannon on board.

The last voyage of the San Diego

cruising off the coast. Its intentions were clear, because its captain had already plundered several junks laden with precious goods. What cheek! In order to put an end to the brazen behavior, the governor of Manila decided to attack the enemy ship at once. Since there were no suitable Spanish warships in the vicinity, they decided to convert the *San Diego* for the task. The necessary arrangements were hastily made.

In those days a merchant ship was only lightly armed – just sufficiently to be able to repulse a pirate attack. The galleon was also laden with cannon, ammunition and weapons of all kinds. Soldiers, including a large number of Japanese mercenaries who offered their services for money, went on board. And so did the aristocratic citizens of Manila, and finally even the commander, the admiral. Unfortunately the admiral had very little idea of sailing, and none at all of the problems of fighting a battle at sea. Ultimately the *San Diego*, 131 feet long and with a crew of almost 500 and 14 cannon on board, was hopelessly overloaded. Things were bound to go wrong!

On December 14th, 1600 the two ships faced each other in the wide bay off Manila. For the *San Diego* the day ended in a disastrous defeat. She sank in the ocean waters while the *Mauritius* was only slightly damaged and was able to get away.

The Dutch equipped a fleet with the aim of sailing round the world and spying on the Spanish enemy.

Two years after it set sail, the fleet reached Manila and began to plunder the ships sailing past.

The peaceful merchant ship *San Diego* was equipped as a warship in order to drive off the Dutch. But the *San Diego* was defeated in the sea battle and sank.

Expedition to the Sa

Is this another part of the ship, or only a coral reef?

For an expedition to be successful, careful preparation is essential. It cannot take place at short notice; you need a lot of time, patience and expert knowledge.

Franck Goddio and his team of scientists knew this all too well. And so they spent a long time gathering together and studying all the useful information about the loss of the *San Diego*. There were accounts by those who survived the disaster and other interesting reports. But where should they start looking for the treasure? The seabed in that region is very uneven and full of coral reefs, many of them the size of a wrecked ship. This meant that electronic sonar equipment was useless. Do you remember? Sonar searches for and finds uneven areas on the flat seabed. A large number of silhouettes which could have been the *San Diego* turned out to be

n Diego

A catamaran makes a very good research ship. It has a shallow draft which makes it suitable for use in shallow water. And because of its twin keels it usually lies quietly in the water, even if the waves are quite choppy.

After more than 400 years a bronze cannon of the *San Diego* re-emerges from the ocean.

hills of coral when the divers looked at them more closely. What a disappointment! A special measuring instrument brought new hope, because it could find and show the location of metals containing iron. It is called a magnetometer. In the case of the *San Diego*, scientists had calculated that over 1,100 lbs of iron must be lying on the bottom of the sea.

The Kaimiloa, the research catamaran, patiently combed a predetermined area measuring about 1.9 x 1.6 miles. Then, at last, after searching without results for four weeks, a happy diver announced that the *San Diego* had been found! It lay at a depth of 174 feet. That is about the height of a 20-story house. Now they would need to be patient. All their scientific research had to be stopped temporarily because the typhoon season had begun. They could expect heavy rainfall and violent storms before long. And in any case, there was still a lot of preparatory work to do. Diving to explore a wreck is a new adventure.

The research ship, a 157-foot tug with a comfortable working platform at the stern, lies at anchor above the wreck of the *San Diego*.

Diving at a depth of 174 feet is no joke – and so a two-man submarine is available to help.

The expedition starts

In January 1992 they were ready to start at last. Like Sleeping Beauty, the *San Diego* had been awakened after 400 years. The divers were overwhelmed by their first encounter: the entire wreck had been transformed into a huge, magnificently colored coral reef. The ship seemed to have been fully absorbed into its natural environment. The divers' powerful lamps lit up dark caves from which startled Moray eels gazed back at them in alarm, their mouths dangerously wide open. Moray eels are found in tropical waters. They look like eels and can grow up to a length of 4 feet 11 inches. These ever-hungry predators have teeth which are as sharp as knives. All divers are afraid of them. Swarms of brightly colored fish flitted through the cone of light past the frogmen. The total silence was both mysterious and frightening. What would they find here in the next days and weeks, in the semi-darkness of the deep? What treasures were on board the proud galleon when it sank

Expedition to the San Diego

Generations of Moray eels have made their home in the wreck of the *San Diego*. The exploration and salvage of the ship soon led to conflicts between the divers and the resident population.

The ship has become a coral reef which provides a habitat for numerous sea-dwelling creatures.

to the depths not far from the shore? But first of all, the divers were captivated by the unspoilt natural environment. Corals are tiny living creatures which form a skeleton by emitting lime, the so-called coral colony. The hollows and branches provide a nutritional basis and habitat for countless brightly colored fish. Crabs and starfish can be found here beside mussels, sea urchins and other mollusks. Fat plants and sea anemones float back and forth in the current. They are constantly on the move and seem to be waving at the curious divers. The water is clear and clean. Quite different from a harbor basin or a bay polluted by industrial effluent! Each of the divers in turn thinks of the drowned sailors. Over the years, the sea has created a magnificent grave for them!

Fish are the divers' constant companions during the excavations.

Once completely cleared the hull of he San Diego can also be studied.

Each diver had his own cage in a different color, weighted down with lead. He could put the objects he had found inside it, stored in plastic bags. At regular intervals the cages were hauled back up on deck. Once they were there they were carefully rinsed with fresh water, numbered and listed on what are known as find cards.

Exploring the galleon

The next days were filled with new, unaccustomed tasks. This time the excavation team consisted of 32 experts, including 18 experienced divers. They could work on the wreck for about 30 minutes, after which the slow decompression phase began as they returned to the surface. On board the base ship, the staff monitored the situation carefully to ensure that the diving times were observed and that the oxygen supply functioned properly. The smallest error could have serious – possibly even fatal – results.

Closer examination revealed that the wreck had broken into two sections when it hit the hilly seabed. The divers discovered some bronze cannon and two large anchors. Stones lay piled up on all sides, hiding the precious finds. They were the so-called ballast stones. The belly of the *San Diego* was full of them in order to ensure that the ship lay deep enough in the water to be stable while sailing. Like an umbilical cord, tubes and lines from the base ship provided the unusual workplace on the seabed with air for breathing and electricity. This meant that all kinds of useful equipment, such as powerful underwater pumps and floodlights could be used.

Those who imagine that hundreds of years later they will find a wooden treasure chest on the seabed, filled with gold and silver items, will be sadly disappointed. Wood would have rotted long ago and been eaten by the worms. The treasures would be carried away or covered with sand by the constant movement of the water, such as the currents. We know that wood is destroyed in water through contact with oxygen. Only when enough sand, mud and other encrustations cover the wreck will it be fairly well protected from decay. Metals containing iron are attacked by the salt water – we say that they corrode. Only precious metals like gold and silver can withstand environmental influences.

Most of the pitchers found at the beginning of the expedition were buried beneath the sand and sediment. Rock-dwellers such as barnacles and marine worms had colo-

The pumps clear the debris out of the way. Once the material has been sucked up it falls onto a large coarse sieve, where the divers can sort out the first small objects.

Expedition to the San Diego

nized the bellies of the pitchers. An aggressive Moray eel refused to be evicted from its lovely, safe home inside the pitcher. It defended its territory furiously. The divers had to be careful, because the sting of the brilliantly camouflaged scorpion fish can also be very painful. Finally, however, all resistance was in vain. At the end of the expedition 800 pitchers of various shapes and sizes saw the light of day once more. On board the *San Diego* they had been used in various ways. As their name indicates, olives and oil were stored in the so-called Spanish olive pitchers with no handles. Gunpowder for the cannons, firearms and pistols were stored in grey, coarse powder vessels. Containers for food and water were mostly very beautifully decorated. There were also a number of large pitchers which were supposed to protect precious trading goods, such as Chinese porcelain, gold and silver jewelry from damage. The holds seem to have been virtually full of the coveted porcelain. Time and again, the divers found themselves gazing once more at the famous blue color. They sometimes found plates, delicate pitchers, bottles with long necks and dishes – a total of more than 1,000 items. Many of them were broken, but even completely undamaged finds found their way into in the nets and baskets of the divers – after more than 400 years on the seabed. What a catch!

Whenever possible the dives were accompanied by a little two-man submarine. Franck Goddio operated it. He remained under water for hours at a time, making notes

The stern of the ship is uncovered: The thick layer of ballast stones is removed one by one and finds, such as pitchers, porcelain and weapons, are salvaged.

From 7 a.m. everybody is hard at work at the site where the *San Diego* was found: archaeologists, submarine engineers and robots meet up.

and supervising the divers' work. He could talk directly to the team on board the base ship; if there was an emergency he could surface immediately, because he did not have to observe the decompression times.

The divers use hand signals to communicate with each other. There is also a small diving robot. Its pincer-like arms are fixed to its sides and it can carry out time-consuming or dangerous tasks. The divers are delighted to accept any help there is. Excavations are always a time-consuming undertaking, but even more so under water. It is a matter of carefully removing a particular surface layer by layer. But removing anything inevitably spoils its original appearance. New, unknown things are revealed. That is why it is essential to record the initial situation as it was first found. This is done by taking photos or drawing and labeling the finds on the spot. Only at the end of an excavation will the overall picture be complete, or the various hypotheses will be confirmed or refuted.

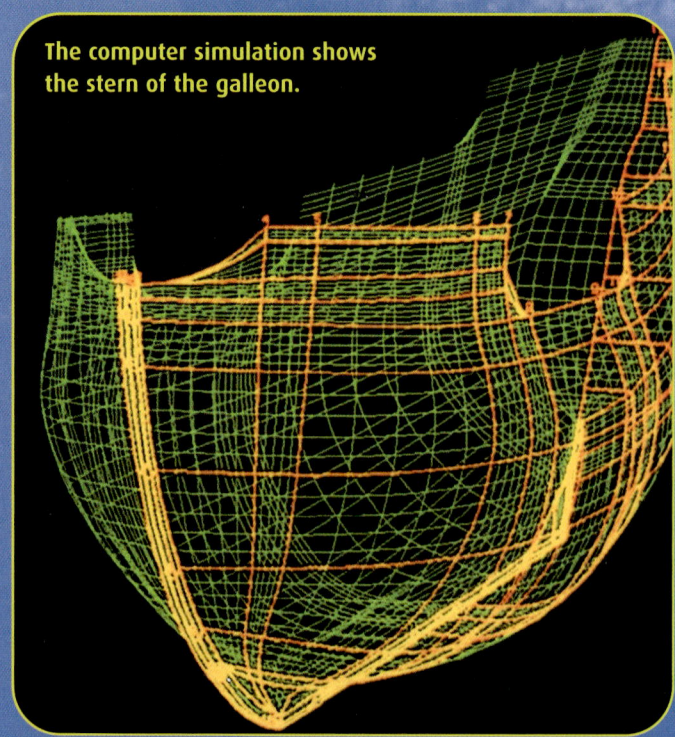

The computer simulation shows the stern of the galleon.

Expedition to the San Diego

Salvaging the cannons

What secrets does the *San Diego* still hold in store for us? Could this be its weapons and cannon?
The team decided to bring the cannon – all 14 magnificent specimens – to Manila and to continue the investigation there.

1 But at the moment they are still lying peacefully at a depth of 164 feet under the sea! To lift them a 230-foot tug with an extremely strong crane anchors above the site of the find. Another camera team and curious film people are watching to see what happens.

2 The divers have secured the barrel of the cannon with two slings made of rope. The crane slowly begins to heave its heavy load up to the surface.

3 A mixture of water and sand gushes out of its barrel when it reaches the surface. Its arrival on deck is greeted with applause.

4 Gradually the finds are being lined up. Here they are – simple long cannon, some which are slightly shorter and are marked with the coat of arms of the King of Spain, and nearby another example, with the year 1598 engraved on it. There is also a Portuguese weapon for hurling stone cannonballs. Clearly a number of foundries in Spain and Portugal had contributed their skills to the arming of the *San Diego*!

5 When the exciting day draws to a close the cannon which have been salvaged weigh a total of 13.5 tonnes, the combined weight of about ten cars. Further finds of weapons prove that there must have been Japanese and Chinese soldiers on board in the form of mercenaries. You can see this clearly because of certain items of equipment, especially their helmets. In the area around the rear decking the divers discover luxurious utensils belonging to the captain and the officers: exquisite dinner services made of finest Chinese porcelain, silver plates, goblets and drinking vessels, and a rosary made of ivory beads with gold spacers. The divers repeatedly also found human skeletons. Some of them were brought to the surface and released for medical investigations. And some of them were left on the seabed, and at the end of the expedition they will be covered in sand again and left to rest in peace once more.

Who owns the treasure?

Both scientists and adventurers are searching for lost treasure throughout the world's oceans. But they are not allowed to keep what they find.

International laws and agreements lay down precisely who such salvaged treasures from the sea belong to. Franck Goddio and the EUROPEAN INSTITUTE FOR UNDERWATER ARCHAEOLOGY, which he founded, carry out every expedition, from the planning to the conclusion, in cooperation with the governments of the countries concerned. The finds are later exhibited in the museums of the country and sometimes in other countries. There they are protected from further decay. As witnesses of past centuries and millennia they should be made available to as many interested viewers as possible, hopefully for all time. Who knows? Maybe one day you will rediscover some old friends from this book, in a special exhibition in the National Museum of Cairo, or in Alexandria or Manila?